THE WOMAN'S WALLET SHOULDN'T JUST BE "STYLISH" BUT IT SHOULD BE "STACKED"!

50K PLANNER Copyright © 2022
All rights reserved— Davronia "Val" Scarbrough

No part of this book may be reproduced or transmitted in any form or by any means, graphic, electronic, or mechanical, including photocopying, recording, taping, or by information storage retrieval system without the written permission of the publisher.

Please direct all copyright inquiries to:
scarvw1@gmail.com

Hardback ISBN: 978-0-9995498-7-2

Cover and Interior Design: Scarbroughed Publications

Printed in the United States of America.

Breaking The 50k Ceiling
🔵🔵🔵

Starting with
$1,000
@
4.05% Interest monthly

Monthly Savings of
$1031.49
for
3.5 years
=

"Ceiling Broken"

TODAY MY FINANCIAL JOURNAL TO SUCCESS STARTS...

> Consistentcy is the magic formula! To accomplish success in any area and financial goals are no different, you must take the approach of "Constant".

SET THE MONEY GOAL FOR 2022

$ _____

50K WOKE MOMENT!

AM I READY FOR THE PAIN OF GROWTH?

UNFILTERED
"No make-up"

UNFILTERED - MY REAL TAKE ON MY FINANCIAL PICTURE

THINGS I REGRET NOT DOING IN THE LAST 5-YRS REGARDING MY FINANCES

WHAT MISINFORMATION HAVE I RECEIVED THAT I DECLARED TO BE WISDOM

ARE YOU AFRAID OF BIG NUMBERS?

Self-Realization "Challenge"

Do I self dive financially?	Taking a different route in my financial picture scares me!	What would my life nonfiction book be titled?	How passionate am I to live in financial Wisdom?	Is my inner circle embodied with great Wealth?
If my money was a Movie, what would the title be?	I like to try new cuisine	Have you ever been to a Ballet?	Have you ever spent 5k on a vacation?	Have you ever invested in a collectible art piece?
Today am I able to blueprint my financial house.	Do I have a great relationship with money?	Do I have a financial accountability partner?	Do I Have A Passport?	Have I ever had a housekeeper?
Does spending 5K on one item scare me?	Do I have at least 5 financial books in my library?	Have you ever paid over $500 for a dinner for 4?	Do I go outside my comfort zone?	Am I moved emotionally when it comes to money?
Do I have more than 2 streams of income coming into my home?	Am I of the mindset that owning a business only will make me wealthy?	I Make time for exercise	Do I read one financial article a week?	Do I Watch the sunset?
I have visited a museum	I find myself chasing dreams	I have ridden 1st Class on a airplane	I like doing Nothing!	Do I live in my dream home today?

 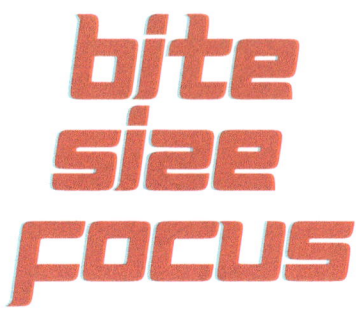

CRYPTOCURRENCY INVESTMENT
&
TRADITIONAL INVESTMENTS

Set an amount for each month. Within the next 6 months I will meet the goal of….

Month 1 Amount: $_____

Month 2 Amount: $_____

Month 3 Amount: $_____

Month 4 Amount: $_____

Month 5 Amount: $_____

Month 6 Amount: $_____

How I plan to employ what I learned...
Action Plan

Good Morning Self

Daily CONFESSION

I am a shark in business, and I always win on every deal. I'm irresistibly attractive to wealthy people - they want to help me out and invest their money with my money. My wealth is progressing every day, and I'm meeting all my financial goals. I have the resources and finances to operate above and beyond what most people can imagine, and it comes easy to me. I have a constant flow of fresh money ideas for real estate and investments that keep me ahead of the curve - there's no fear when it comes to cryptocurrencies either!

I enjoy investing in cryptocurrency, gold, silver, and stocks. I am healthy and wealthy because of my positive choices. I come against negative thoughts about making money, thoughts deposited in me through fear. I declare full recovery of things I lost knowingly, unwillingly, and that were stolen from me.

Today, I set my heart and life to great wealth!
I will break the 50K financial ceiling!

FIRESIDE CHAT NOTES 🔥

50k Planner Month 1

We have to plan for our 50k Goal

I Made It To Our Monthly Meeting!

My Top Priorities For Investing This Month

- ○
- ○
- ○

How much did I give or sow into someone's life this month?

I have to make daily nutrition a goal

Breakfast	No Later Than 9:am
Lunch	No Later Than 2:pm
Dinner	No Later Than 7:30pm
Snack	Eat 3 healthy stacks

FINANCIAL WISDOM PLAN

Crypto Investment Month 1

S M T W T F S

The Days I Invest:

Income Goal:

Interest Goal:

List of Exchanges	Amount

Goal for this week	Amount	Due

Did I meet my Income Goal:

Did I meet my Interest Goal:

Embrace Savings!
Savings is a great part of a strong financial picture.

Savings Plan Month 1

My Goals	Amount Saved This Month
Mutual Fund	
529b Education Fund	
401k Fund	
Christmas Savings	

Overall Savings Balance:

Did I put something in savings weekly:

I made a one time investment this month in a savings:

I met my savings goal this month:

Goal Amount To Save This Month:

Notes:

The Market Is There To Work For Me!

Stock Market Investment Month 1

S M T W T F S

Day I Invest

My Goals	Amount Invested This Month
Money Market	
ROTH IRA	
STOCKS	
FOREX	

Overall Stock Balance:

Did I put something in the market weekly:

I made a one time investment this month into one of my investment accounts:

I met my investment goal this month:

Goal Amount To Invest This Month:

Notes:

I spoke to my "Accountability Partner"

This month I need to talk about...

- _____
- _____
- _____
- _____
- _____

"My Take Away"

Notes

End of the month
15-minute review of my financial growth.

_____
_____
_____
_____
_____
_____
_____
_____
_____
_____
_____
_____
_____
_____
_____

FIRESIDE CHAT NOTES 🔥

50k Planner Month 2

We have to plan for our 50k Goal.

I Made It To Our Monthly Meeting!

My Top Priorities For Investing This Month

How much did I give or sow into someone's life this month?

I have to make daily nutrition a goal.

Breakfast	No Later Than 9:am
Lunch	No Later Than 2:pm
Dinner	No Later Than 7:30pm
Snack	Eat 3 healthy stacks

FINANCIAL WISDOM PLAN

Crypto Investment Month 2

S M T W T F S

The Days I Invest:

Income Goal:

Interest Goal:

List of Exchanges	Amount

Goal for this week	Amount	Due

Did I meet my Income Goal:

Did I meet my Interest Goal:

Embrace Savings!
Savings is a great part of a strong financial picture.

Savings Plan Month 2

S M T W T F S

Date:

My Goals	Amount Saved This Month
Mutual Fund	
529b Education Fund	
401k Fund	
Christmas Savings	

Overall Savings Balance:

Did I put something in savings weekly:

I made a one time investment this month in a savings:

I met my savings goal this month:

Goal Amount To Save This Month:

Notes:

The Market Is There To Work For Me!

Stock Market Investment Month 2

S M T W T F S

Day I Invest

My Goals	Amount Invested This Month
Money Market	
ROTH IRA	
STOCKS	
FOREX	

- Overall Stock Balance:
- Did I put something in the market weekly:
- I made a one time investment this month into one of my investment accounts:
- I met my investment goal this month:
- Goal Amount To Invest This Month:

Notes:

I spoke to my "Accountability Partner"

This month I need to talk about...

- _____
- _____
- _____
- _____
- _____

"My Take Away"

Notes

End of the month 15-minute review of my financial growth.

50K TIP!

Great wealth is created by the "wisdom" decisions you make about your money! You don't want to make money only, you want to "MULTIPLY" it!

3rd Month

to

Financial

Freedom

FIRESIDE CHAT NOTES

50k Planner Month 3

We have to plan for our 50k Goal.

I Made It To Our Monthly Meeting!

_____
_____
_____
_____
_____
_____
_____
_____

My Top Priorities For Investing This Month

○ _____
○ _____
○ _____

How much did I give or sow into someone's life this month?

_____
_____
_____
_____

I have to make daily nutrition a goal.

Breakfast	No Later Than 9:am
Lunch	No Later Than 2:pm
Dinner	No Later Than 7:30pm
Snack	Eat 3 healthy stacks

FINANCIAL WISDOM PLAN

Crypto Investment Month 3

S M T W T F S

The Days I Invest:

Income Goal:

Interest Goal:

List of Exchanges	Amount

Goal for this week	Amount	Due

Did I meet my Income Goal:

Did I meet my Interest Goal:

Embrace Savings!
Savings is a great part of a strong financial picture.

Savings Plan Month 3

S M T W T F S

Date:

My Goals	Amount Saved This Month
Mutual Fund	
529b Education Fund	
401k Fund	
Christmas Savings	

Overall Savings Balance:

Did I put something in savings weekly:

I made a one time investment this month in a savings:

I met my savings goal this month:

Goal Amount To Save This Month:

Notes:

The Market Is There To Work For Me!

Stock Market Investment Month 3

S M T W T F S

Day I Invest

My Goals	Amount Invested This Month
Money Market	
ROTH IRA	
STOCKS	
FOREX	

Overall Stock Balance:

Did I put something in the market weekly:

I made a one time investment this month into one of my investment accounts:

I met my investment goal this month:

Goal Amount To Invest This Month:

Notes:

I spoke to my "Accountability Partner"

This month I need to talk about...

- _____
- _____
- _____
- _____
- _____

"My Take Away"

Notes

End of the month 15-minute review of my financial growth.

"Reward" yourself without "Guilt"!

Investment Garden
"The Over & Above Challenge"

I Invested $5.00 in -------- Today	I Invested $15.00 in -------- Today	I Invested $25.00 in -------- Today	I Invested $30.00 in -------- Today	I Invested $35.00 in -------- Today
I Invested $40.00 in -------- Today	I Invested $45.00 in -------- Today	I Invested $50.00 in -------- Today	I Invested $55.00 in -------- Today	I Invested $15.00 in -------- Today
I AM PROUD OF MY PROGRESS	I Invested $65.00 in -------- Today	I Invested $75.00 in -------- Today	I Invested $150.00 in -------- Today	I Invested $175.00 in -------- Today
I Invested $180.00 in -------- Today	I Invested $200.00 in -------- Today	MY INTEREST RECEIVED AS OF TODAY ---------- ✓	I Invested $15.00 in -------- Today	I Invested $15.00 in -------- Today
I Invested $25.00 in -------- Today	I Invested $35.00 in -------- Today	I Invested $75.00 in -------- Today	I Invested $15.00 in -------- Today	
My Biggest Investment yet! _____	MY INTEREST RECEIVED AS OF TODAY ---------- ✓		**My Total Interest Gain** _____	**My Total =** _____

FIRESIDE CHAT NOTES

50k Planner Month 4

We have to plan for our 50k Goal.

I Made It To Our Monthly Meeting!

_____
_____
_____
_____
_____
_____
_____
_____
_____
_____

My Top Priorities For Investing This Month

○ _____
○ _____
○ _____

How much did I give or sow into someone's life this month?

_____
_____
_____
_____

I have to make daily nutrition a goal.

Breakfast	No Later Than 9:am
Lunch	No Later Than 2:pm
Dinner	No Later Than 7:30pm
Snack	Eat 3 healthy stacks

FINANCIAL WISDOM PLAN

Crypto Investment Month 4

S M T W T F S

The Days I Invest:

Income Goal:

Interest Goal:

List of Exchanges	Amount

Goal for this week	Amount	Due

Did I meet my Income Goal:

Did I meet my Interest Goal:

Embrace Savings!
Savings is a great part of a strong financial picture.

Savings Plan Month 4

S M T W T F S

Date:

My Goals	Amount Saved This Month
Mutual Fund	
529b Education Fund	
401k Fund	
Christmas Savings	

Overall Savings Balance:

Did I put something in savings weekly:

I made a one time investment this month in a savings:

I met my savings goal this month:

Goal Amount To Save This Month:

Notes:

The Market Is There To Work For Me!

Stock Market Investment Month 4

S M T W T F S

Day I Invest

My Goals	Amount Invested This Month
Money Market	
ROTH IRA	
STOCKS	
FOREX	

Overall Stock Balance:

Did I put something in the market weekly:

I made a one time investment this month into one of my investment accounts:

I met my investment goal this month:

Goal Amount To Invest This Month:

Notes:

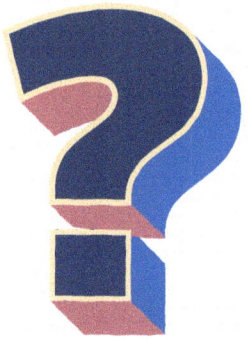

I spoke to my "Accountability Partner"

This month I need to talk about...

- _____
- _____
- _____
- _____
- _____

"My Take Away"

Notes
_____
_____
_____
_____

End of the month
15-minute review of my financial growth.

_____
_____
_____
_____
_____
_____
_____
_____
_____
_____
_____
_____
_____
_____
_____

"Success" is going to come from tracking the "Progress".

FIRESIDE CHAT NOTES 🔥

50k Planner Month 5

We have to plan for our 50k Goal.

I Made It To Our Monthly Meeting!

My Top Priorities For Investing This Month

- ⃝ _____
- ⃝ _____
- ⃝ _____

How much did I give or sow into someone's life this month?

I have to make daily nutrition a goal.

Breakfast	No Later Than 9:am
Lunch	No Later Than 2:pm
Dinner	No Later Than 7:30pm
Snack	Eat 3 healthy stacks

FINANCIAL WISDOM PLAN

Crypto Investment Month 5

S M T W T F S

The Days I Invest:

Income Goal:

Interest Goal:

List of Exchanges	Amount

Goal for this week	Amount	Due

Did I meet my Income Goal:

Did I meet my Interest Goal:

Embrace Savings!
Savings is a great part of a strong financial picture.

Savings Plan Month 5

S M T W T F S

Date:

My Goals	Amount Saved This Month
Mutual Fund	
529b Education Fund	
401k Fund	
Christmas Savings	

Overall Savings Balance:

Did I put something in savings weekly:

I made a one time investment this month in a savings:

I met my savings goal this month:

Goal Amount To Save This Month:

Notes:

The Market Is There To Work For Me!

Stock Market Investment Month 5

S M T W T F S

Days I Invest

My Goals	Amount Invested This Month
Money Market	
ROTH IRA	
STOCKS	
FOREX	

Overall Stock Balance:

Did I put something in the market weekly:

I made a one time investment this month into one of my investment accounts:

I met my investment goal this month:

Goal Amount To Invest This Month:

Notes:

I spoke to my "Accountability Partner"

This month I need to talk about...

- _____
- _____
- _____
- _____
- _____

"My Take Away"

Notes
_____
_____
_____
_____

End of the month 15-minute review of my financial growth.

FREEING UP MONEY

Freeing up your money has to be the primary "Goal". The formula below is the perfect way to help you achieve your financial goal of "FREE" flowing money!
Don't delay, put the formula to work.
With this goal in mind, you'll be able to make wise decisions about your finances and grow your wealth steadily!

Within the next month I will.............

Grow my personal bank account (s) by_____ percent to equal $_____ Grow my business bank account (s) by _____ percent to equal $_____ .

(How will I invest the extra money?)

LET'S GO!

Formula:

#1 Pay off the least amount of debt within the next 30-days;

#2 roll that money over that you use to payoff last debt to the next debt to be paid off within 30-days

#3 repeat until all debts are eliminated or under control.

AUGUST

Getting comfortable with investing

—

6th Month to Financial Freedom

FIRESIDE CHAT NOTES

50k Planner Month 6

We have to plan for our 50k Goal.

I Made It To Our Monthly Meeting!

_____

_____

_____

_____

_____

_____

_____

My Top Priorities For Investing This Month

○ _____

○ _____

○ _____

How much did I give or sow into someone's life this month?

_____

_____

_____

_____

I have to make daily nutrition a goal.

Breakfast	No Later Than 9:am
Lunch	No Later Than 2:pm
Dinner	No Later Than 7:30pm
Snack	Eat 3 healthy stacks

FINANCIAL WISDOM PLAN

Crypto Investment Month 6

S M T W T F S

The Days I Invest:

Income Goal:

Interest Goal:

List of Exchanges	Amount

Goal for this week	Amount	Due

Did I meet my Income Goal:

Did I meet my Interest Goal:

Embrace Savings!
Savings is a great part of a strong financial picture.

Savings Plan Month 6

S M T W T F S

Days I Invest:

My Goals	Amount Saved This Month
Mutual Fund	
529b Education Fund	
401k Fund	
Christmas Savings	

- Overall Savings Balance:
- Did I put something in savings weekly:
- I made a one time investment this month in a savings:
- I met my savings goal this month:
- Goal Amount To Save This Month:

Notes:

The Market Is There To Work For Me!

Stock Market Investment Month 6

S M T W T F S

Days I Invest:

My Goals	Amount Invested This Month
Money Market	
ROTH IRA	
STOCKS	
FOREX	

Overall Stock Balance:

Did I put something in the market weekly

I made a one time investment this month into one of my investment accounts

I met my investment goal this month

Goal Amount To Invest This Month:

Notes:

I spoke to my "Accountability Partner"

This month I need to talk about...

- _____
- _____
- _____
- _____
- _____

"My Take Away"

Notes

End of the month 15-minute review of my financial growth.

OUR INNER CIRCLE REPRESENTS 10% DIFFERENCE!

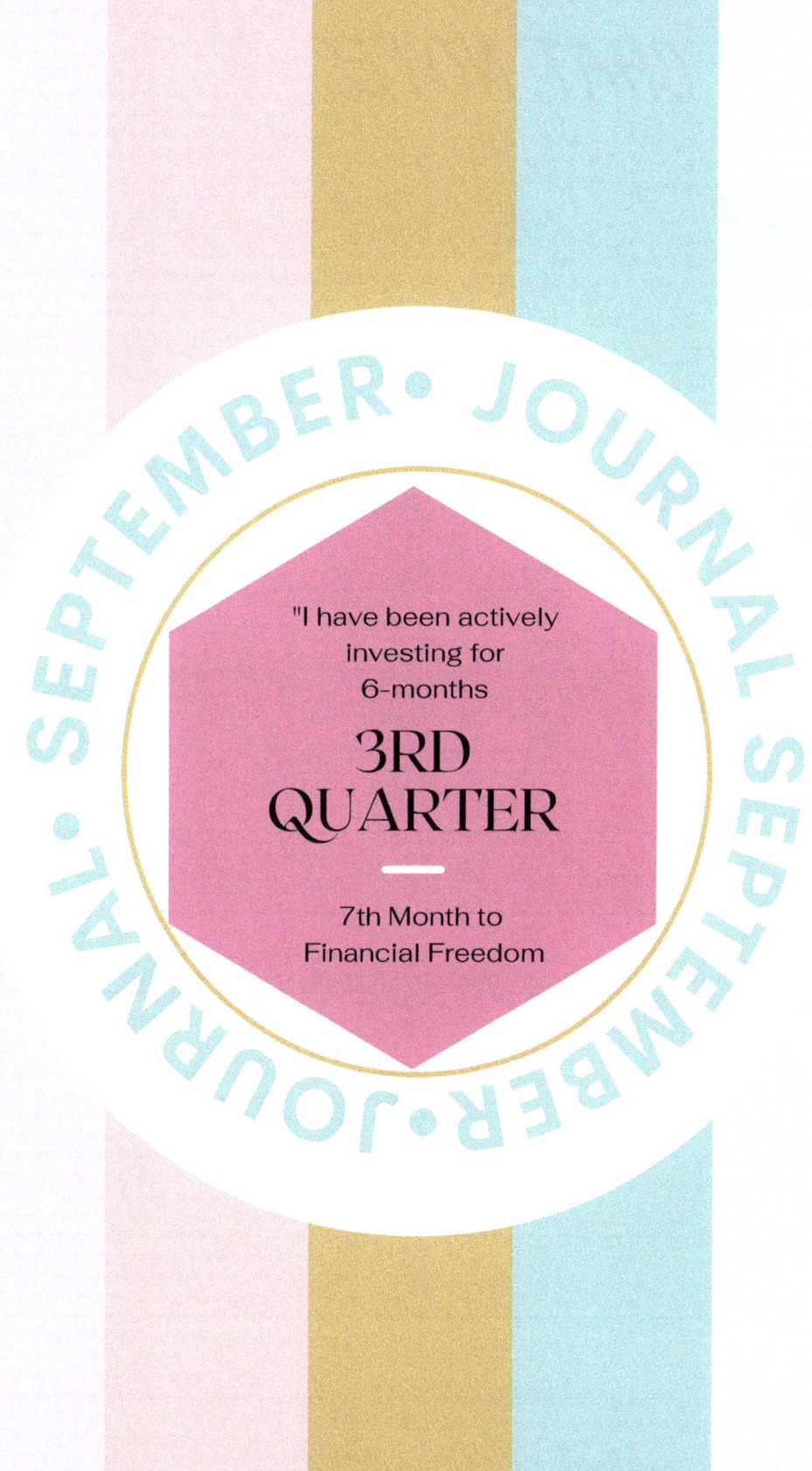

FIRESIDE CHAT NOTES

50k Planner Month 7

We have to plan for our 50k Goal.

I Made It To Our Monthly Meeting!

_____
_____
_____
_____
_____
_____
_____
_____
_____

My Top Priorities For Investing This Month

○ _____
○ _____
○ _____

How much did I give or sow into someone's life this month?

_____
_____
_____
_____
_____

I have to make daily nutrition a goal.

Breakfast	No Later Than 9:am
Lunch	No Later Than 2:pm
Dinner	No Later Than 7:30pm
Snack	Eat 3 healthy stacks

FINANCIAL WISDOM PLAN

Crypto Investment Month 7

S M T W T F S

The Days I Invest:

Income Goal:

Interest Goal:

List of Exchanges	Amount

Goal for this week	Amount	Due

Did I meet my Income Goal:

Did I meet my Interest Goal:

Embrace Savings!
Savings is a great part of a strong financial picture.

Savings Plan Month 7

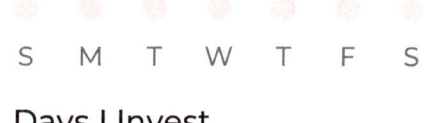

S M T W T F S

Days I Invest

My Goals	Amount Saved This Month
Mutual Fund	
529b Education Fund	
401k Fund	
Christmas Savings	

Overall Savings Balance:

Did I put something in savings weekly:

I made a one time investment this month in a savings:

I met my savings goal this month:

Goal Amount To Save This Month:

Notes:

The Market Is There To Work For Me!

Stock Market Investment Month 7

S M T W T F S

Days I Invest

My Goals	Amount Invested This Month
Money Market	
ROTH IRA	
STOCKS	
FOREX	

Overall Stock Balance:

Did I put something in the market weekly:

I made a one time investment this month into one of my investment accounts:

I met my investment goal this month:

Goal Amount To Invest This Month:

Notes:

I spoke to my "Accountability Partner"

This month I need to talk about...

- _____
- _____
- _____
- _____
- _____

"My Take Away"

Notes
_____
_____
_____
_____

End of the month 15-minute review of my financial growth.

There is nothing wrong with being an adversary to your plan.
What is the one thing
that could hinder you from accomplishing your goal?

Write SOLUTIONS
(i.e. household expense, leisure habits, excessively eating out, a lack of innovation)

You always want to put
a demand on yourself.
*

Be Solution Oriented!

FIRESIDE CHAT NOTES

50k Planner Month 8

We have to plan for our 50k Goal.

I Made It To Our Monthly Meeting!

_____
_____
_____
_____
_____
_____
_____
_____

My Top Priorities For Investing This Month

○ _____
○ _____
○ _____

How much did I give or sow into someone's life this month?

_____
_____
_____
_____

I have to make daily nutrition a goal.

Breakfast	No Later Than 9:am
Lunch	No Later Than 2:pm
Dinner	No Later Than 7:30pm
Snack	Eat 3 healthy stacks

FINANCIAL WISDOM PLAN

Crypto Investment Month 8

S M T W T F S

The Days I Invest:

Income Goal:

Interest Goal:

List of Exchanges	Amount

Goal for this week	Amount	Due

Did I meet my Income Goal:

Did I meet my Interest Goal:

Embrace Savings!
Savings is a great part of a strong financial picture

Savings Plan Month 8

My Goals	Amount Saved This Month
Mutual Fund	
529b Education Fund	
401k Fund	
Christmas Savings	

Overall Savings Balance:

Did I put something in savings weekly:

I made a one time investment this month in a savings:

I met my savings goal this month:

Goal Amount To Save This Month:

Notes:

The Market Is There To Work For Me!

Stock Market Investment Month 8

S M T W T F S

Days I Invest

My Goals	Amount Invested This Month
Money Market	
ROTH IRA	
STOCKS	
FOREX	

Overall Stock Balance:

Did I put something in the market weekly:

I made a one time investment this month into one of my investment accounts:

I met my investment goal this month:

Goal Amount To Invest This Month:

Notes:

I spoke to my "Accountability Partner"

This month I need to talk about...

- _____
- _____
- _____
- _____
- _____

"My Take Away"

Notes

End of the month 15-minute review of my financial growth.

_____
_____
_____
_____
_____
_____
_____
_____
_____
_____
_____
_____
_____
_____
_____
_____
_____

50K TIP!

SET A REALISTIC PERCENTAGE OF YOUR INCOME TOWARD INVESTMENTS & HARD ASSETS EACH MONTH!
(Examples: Digital Real Estate, Real Estate, Silver, Gold, etc.)

NOVEMBER!

The holiday season will challenge your financial growth

STAY FOCUSED

50k Planner
Month 9

We have to plan for our 50k Goal.

I Made It To Our Monthly Meeting!

_____
_____
_____
_____
_____
_____
_____
_____

My Top Priorities For Investing This Month

○ _____
○ _____
○ _____

How much did I give or sow into someone's life this month?

_____
_____
_____

I have to make daily nutrition a goal.

Breakfast	No Later Than 9:am
Lunch	No Later Than 2:pm
Dinner	No Later Than 7:30pm
Snack	Eat 3 healthy stacks

FINANCIAL WISDOM PLAN

Crypto Investment Month 9

S M T W T F S

The Days I Invest:

Income Goal:

Interest Goal:

List of Exchanges	Amount

Goal for this week	Amount	Due

Did I meet my Income Goal:

Did I meet my Interest Goal:

Embrace Savings!
Savings is a great part of a strong financial picture.

Savings Plan Month 9

S M T W T F S

Days I Invest

My Goals	Amount Saved This Month
Mutual Fund	
529b Education Fund	
401k Fund	
Christmas Savings	

Overall Savings Balance:

Did I put something in savings weekly:

I made a one time investment this month in a savings:

I met my savings goal this month:

Goal Amount To Save This Month:

Notes:

The Market Is There To Work For Me!

Stock Market Investment Month 9

S M T W T F S

Days I Invest

My Goals	Amount Invested This Month
Money Market	
ROTH IRA	
STOCKS	
FOREX	

Overall Stock Balance:

Did I put something in the market weekly:

I made a one time investment this month into one of my investment accounts:

I met my investment goal this month:

Goal Amount To Invest This Month:

Notes:

I spoke to my "Accountability Partner"

This month I need to talk about...

- _____
- _____
- _____
- _____
- _____

"My Take Away"

Notes
_____
_____
_____
_____

End of the month 15-minute review of my financial growth.

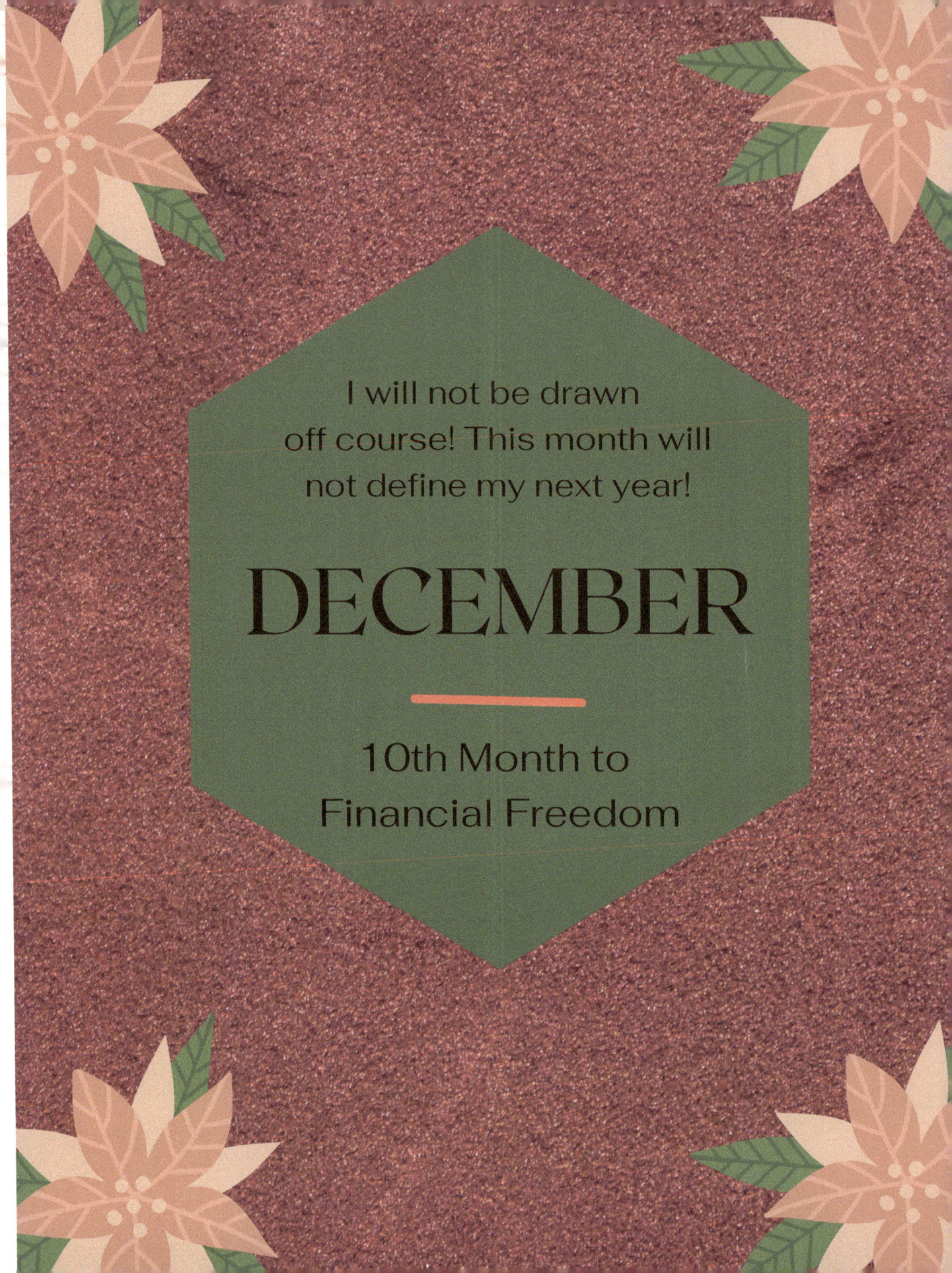

FIRESIDE CHAT NOTES

50k Planner Month 10

We have to plan for our 50k Goal.

I Made It To Our Monthly Meeting!

_____
_____
_____
_____
_____
_____
_____
_____
_____

My Top Priorities For Investing This Month

○ _____
○ _____
○ _____

How much did I give or sow into someone's life this month?

_____
_____
_____
_____

I have to make daily nutrition a goal.

Breakfast	No Later Than 9:am
Lunch	No Later Than 2:pm
Dinner	No Later Than 7:30pm
Snack	Eat 3 healthy stacks

FINANCIAL WISDOM PLAN

Crypto Investment Month 10

S M T W T F S

The Days I Invest:

Income Goal:

Interest Goal:

List of Exchanges	Amount

Goal for this week	Amount	Due

Did I meet my Income Goal:

Did I meet my Interest Goal:

Embrace Savings!
Savings is a great part of a strong financial picture

Savings Plan Month 10

S M T W T F S

Days I Invest

My Goals	Amount Saved This Month
Mutual Fund	
529b Education Fund	
401k Fund	
Christmas Savings Cash Out	

Overall Savings Balance:

Did I put something in savings weekly

I made a one time investment this month in a savings

I met my savings goal this month

Goal Amount To Save This Month:

Notes:

The Market Is There To Work For Me!

Stock Market Investment Month 10

S M T W T F S

Days I Invest

My Goals	Amount Invested This Month
Money Market	
ROTH IRA	
STOCKS	
FOREX	

Overall Stock Balance:

Did I put something in the market weekly:

I made a one time investment this month into one of my investment accounts:

I met my investment goal this month:

Goal Amount To Invest This Month:

Notes:

I spoke to my "Accountability Partner"

This month I need to talk about...

- _____
- _____
- _____
- _____
- _____

"My Take Away"

Notes
_____
_____
_____
_____

End of the month 15-minute review of my financial growth.

Expense Tracker

MONTH: DECEMBER 2022

DATE	ITEM	SPENT	REMAINS

CONGRATULATIONS!!!!!

You Have Completed

10-MONTHS OF FINANCIAL LITERACY

YOU CHANGED THE TRAJECTORY OF YOUR LEGACY!!!